D1614123

THE BALLET BOOK

ANDREW PTAK

THE BALLET BOOK

A YOUNG DANCER'S GUIDE

FOREWORD BY KAREN KAIN

Beaufort Books, Inc.
New York

Library of Congress Cataloging in Publication Data

Ptak, Andrew.
    The ballet book.

    1. Ballet.   I. Title.
GV1787.P77   1984   792.8'2   84-6451
ISBN 0-8253-0230-7

Published in the United States by Beaufort Books, Inc., New York.
First American Edition

Key Porter Books
70 The Esplanade
Toronto, Ontario
Canada   M5E 1R2

Design: Don Fernley
Typesetting: Compeer Typographic Services Limited
Printing and Binding: Sagdos S.p.A.
Printed and bound in Italy

84 85 86 87 6 5 4 3 2 1

To Sarah and Claire

CONTENTS

ACKNOWLEDGEMENTS

No book is produced solely by one person. In the case of this book, the staff and students of the Quinte Dance Centre, a professional ballet school, are to be thanked. In particular, I would like to thank Brian Scott, Artistic Director, who put his many years of ballet experience at my disposal and contributed all of the technical information necessary to produce this book. I would also like to thank Sharon Airhart, Executive Director and a former journalist, who took my original manuscript and made a complex subject understandable.

A further thank you to Ainsley Cyopic and the students who appear in the photographs. Special thanks are due to Meredith Heaney and Alison McCreary, the two students featured in most of the photographs of ballet technique. They contributed many hours in front of the camera.

FOREWORD

B allet skills are passed from generation to generation by teachers who have been dancers themselves. They take great pleasure in passing on their knowledge and experience to you, their student.

This book cannot replace your dance teacher any more than a book in school can replace your English or Math teacher. Use it to review what you have already learned in your classes and to look back on some things that you may have forgotten. You can compare your work with the photographs. They may remind you of corrections you have been given in class.

Remember, classes several times a week are much better than one class a week. Don't be discouraged by the advanced work. When you get to it, you will be ready. Don't try to do advanced exercises without your teacher's help; you will waste your time and you might hurt yourself.

How do you choose a good school? That is a difficult question. Many good teachers belong to The Imperial Society of Teachers of Dancing or the Royal Academy of Dancing. Membership does not guarantee good instruction any more than non-membership guarantees poor instruction. But in order to belong to either organization, the teacher must pass an internationally recognized examination.

Not everyone who wants to dance can become a professional dancer. However, that should not stop you from learning to dance, because you will develop many important skills through your training. You will be an athlete with a sense of grace and style, patient and determined to succeed. And, as a dancer, you will learn to actually feel music, not just hear it as most people do. So whether you want to become a professional dancer or an amateur one, ballet training can help you to become a special kind of person.

There is no rule that says who can be a dancer, or what level you should have achieved by a certain age. You work according to your own skill, at the pace that is right for you and your body. Each person is different and dancers are no exception.

KAREN KAIN,
PRINCIPAL DANCER WITH THE
NATIONAL BALLET OF CANADA

1   HOW BALLET STARTED

Ballet did not suddenly appear one day. It grew slowly over a long period of time. Italy, home of many great artists, was the birthplace of formal dancing. The dances were performed by aristocrats for their own amusement.

What was popular in Italy soon became popular in France. King Louis XIV loved to dance and staged elaborate dances with his attendants at the palace. Eventually, Louis XIV grew too fat and had to stop dancing. He arranged for the performances to continue, however, by paying for the training of professional dancers.

The Académie de Danse, the first school of dance, was founded in 1661. It was at this school that the first five positions of the feet were worked out. As a matter of fact, so many positions were created and named there that French remains the language of ballet all over the world.

At first, all of the dancers were men, but in 1681, women finally appeared on the professional stage, playing minor roles. By the mid-1800s, however, they had completely taken over and were dancing most of the male roles as well. While male dancers lost their importance in Europe, they still had a strong influence in Russia.

In 1738, in St. Petersburg (now Leningrad), French ballet master Jean-Baptiste Landé started a ballet school for the children of servants at the Czar's Court. The Imperial family were great supporters of the school. This school became the world-famous Kirov School.

About 1820, dancers first went *sur la pointe*. When Marie Taglioni, the first ballerina to wear a romantic tutu (long tutu), danced on point in *La Sylphide* in 1832, the great Romantic ballet period had begun.

Although these were major developments, ballet became very stale in most of Europe soon afterward. In Denmark and Russia alone, fine ballets and excellent dancers were produced.

A Frenchman had brought ballet to Russia and, in 1909, a Russian took it back to France, returning the magic and excitement that French ballet had lost. Serge Diaghilev took the Ballets Russes to Paris and introduced his spectacular principal dancer, Vaslav Nijinsky, to the world. Their first performances were an overwhelming success as stories of Nijinsky's great leaps spread throughout Europe. Anna Pavlova, one of the world's most famous ballerinas, was also in this company of dancers.

Before the founding of the Ballets Russes in Europe, and the dramatic changes introduced by its choreographer, Mikhail Fokine, ballet was not considered suitable employment for nice girls. The majority of the dancers were daughters of dancers or from poor families. However, Fokine's choreography and ballet master Enrico Cecchetti's teaching methods changed ballet forever. Their Ballets Russes dancers were graceful and disciplined professional artists, unlike the dumpy ballerinas in corsets that had become common on most stages. Because of the principles introduced by Cecchetti and Fokine, dancers' legs lost their bulging muscles and became more slender.

Over the next fifty years, ballet grew slowly and quietly. New companies were formed and new dances introduced. Many dancers adopted Russian-sounding names in order to be taken seriously in their own countries.

In 1961, Rudolf Nureyev, a dramatic Kirov dancer, left Russia for the Western world. His magnificent leaps and restless energy appealed to many new ballet-goers. They flocked to see him. Dame Margot Fonteyn, one of the greatest ballerinas in England's Royal Ballet, found a "new" career at the age of forty-two as Nureyev's partner. She enjoyed the most glorious days of her career just when everyone thought that it was over.

In 1974, Mikhail Baryshnikov, while on tour in Canada with the Kirov, left that company and joined the American Ballet Theatre.

Ballet is now more popular than ever before, and much of the increased enthusiasm is due to Nureyev and Baryshnikov. Their dramatic Russian style and good looks have attracted and pleased ballet audiences worldwide.

Although ballet is a highly disciplined art and shares this common 300-year-old history, you will find that each ballet company is very different. There is much room for interpretation and differences in style and taste, both in performance and in training.

The three main methods of classical ballet training in use today are Cecchetti, Royal Academy of Dancing and Russian. Although many positions and exercises are held in common, each has slight variations. The photographs in this book are based on the Cecchetti method. The way some of the exercises are performed may differ from the way you are taught, because your school may follow a different method, or your teacher may have a different interpretation.

In performance, national styles and characteristics also differ. The Russians dance with great strength and fluid movement. French dancers prefer elegance. The English style is delicate and subtle. The Danes use brilliant footwork, speed and lightness of movement, and in the United States, dancers are known for their agility and athleticism. Choreographers will add their own styles, too!

The ballets of the Russian Imperial Ballet and Diaghilev's Ballets Russes form the backbone of classical repertoire for nearly every company in the world. However, each company's version will be very different. Ballet schooling, style and the choreographer's own ideas will vary the performance considerably.

Although she is kept busy performing on stages around the world,
Karen Kain still occasionally finds time to teach.

2   THE YEARS OF TRAINING

Although there are no rules about what age a student should be to start ballet or how quickly a student should progress, there are some general guidelines.

Age eight or nine is a good time to start ballet; however, pre-ballet may be started earlier. At this age, muscles are loose and elastic, bones are still pliable, and the brain knows how to coordinate arm and leg movements.

The beginning exercises are aimed at coordinating movement to music. Work begins immediately on two of the most important goals for a dancer to achieve: balance and turnout.

No matter what position a dancer is in, on one leg or two, the body must be balanced over the hips and onto the supporting leg or legs. This is why the *barre* is so important; it is where balance is first developed.

Turnout is the outward rotation of the entire leg in the hip, without moving the hip itself. It enables dancers to turn their legs in opposite directions and to swing a leg high up in the air. To develop and hold turnout takes many years.

After two or three years, more difficult exercises and positions are attempted. The one technique that girls look forward to is going on point. Toes of equal length help. If a student has a long big toe that sticks out ahead of the others, point work could be difficult.

The exercises and positions slowly become more challenging over the next few years. New positions, such as *arabesques*, are attempted, but important work goes on in the positions learned in earlier years. They are performed with more turnout, and the student has the ability to perform them without the *barre*. *Port de bras*, as the movement of the arms is called, becomes increasingly more challenging. A dancer conveys emotion and expression with the arms. Graceful *port de bras*, where the arms move from one position to another while maintaining the line of the body, is very difficult.

The student also develops strength. For the dancer, strength is measured not only in power, but also in stamina. Strength and stamina must be displayed without showing strain.

Although ballet is difficult and muscles may become sore on occasion, especially when attempting new movements, it should never be painful. If it is painful, something may be wrong. Perhaps you are not in the correct position or should not be attempting the exercise at your stage of development.

It may seem that individual classes, positions or exercises have little relationship to one another. But all ballet methods follow a plan that has been developed over hundreds of years.

Each ballet class exercise is directed toward a goal. This goal may be increased turnout, better balance, stronger feet, ankles and legs, looser joints or one of many other qualities needed to dance. Exercises all have a reason to exist, and the order in which they follow one another is important, too.

In the last century, the Italian and Danish dancers began *barre* exercises with high kicks, while the Russians put the kicks at the end of *barre* practice. This is one of the reasons that the Ballets Russes dancers had strong but slender legs, and the Italian and Danish dancers had heavier thighs. So you see, even the sequence of exercises has an important role in dance training.

All of the positions have been planned so that they can be combined, in various sequences, and will flow from one to another in a movement that presents attractive body lines to the audience.

Many schools have an annual performance, which friends and relatives can attend. These performances not only display what you have learned, but are also part of the ballet training that prepares dancers for the stage.

The positions and exercises beginning in Chapter 4 are not the only ones in classical ballet, but they are some of the most important. Each one is like a piece of a jigsaw puzzle. Individually, they may not appear important, but combined with all of the other pieces, they grow into a beautiful picture.

Students watch as their teacher shows the correct arm movement in a back bend.

These students are wearing different types of warm-up clothing.
Left, a woolen bodywarmer; *center*, a leotard and leg warmers;
right, nylon warm-up pants.

3 WHAT TO WEAR

Whether in the classroom or on the stage, dancers wear specially designed clothing. Although some of their clothing may be fashionable from time to time, to a dancer it means much more than looking nice. Each piece of clothing has a job to do.

A leotard and tights are the dancer's basic practice clothing. For classical work, girls usually wear dark navy or black leotards with pink tights. Some schools prefer short socks or colored leotards. Sometimes a short wraparound skirt of sheer material is worn on top of the leotard. Boys usually wear a white T-shirt and black tights.

When the student or dancer begins to exercise, leg warmers are used to help cold muscles warm up more quickly. They are usually taken off when the muscles are warm. Bodywarmers, usually knitted, are sometimes worn during rehearsals when working and waiting periods alternate.

Hair is also part of the dancer's costume. Students and dancers in classical work wear their medium-long hair in buns so that the line of the neck and head can be seen.

Soft shoes are worn by students until they work on point. Made of soft leather or canvas – usually pink for girls and black or white for boys – the shoes are held on firmly by elastic sewn on by the students.

Point shoes, with blocked toes, come without ribbons. They must fit perfectly and the ribbons sewn on just the right way for each dancer. The ribbons cross over and go around the leg three times. The ends must be neatly tucked in. Many dancers dust their shoes with powder so that they are not shiny on stage.

4   THE BASICS

The five basic positions of the feet in classical ballet are learned first, not because they are easy, but because most movements in ballet class begin and end in one of these positions.

At first, these beginning positions will be difficult. Legs are not held naturally with the feet pointing in opposite directions to each other; muscles must be stretched before that can happen.

People are born with different degrees of natural turnout. Ballet exercises increase turnout by stretching the inside muscles of the thigh so that the leg can rotate outward in the hip joint.

Why is turnout important? A leg rotated outward presents an attractive body line to the audience and allows a dancer to move much more freely than would otherwise be possible.

Turnout does not develop quickly but takes time and training.

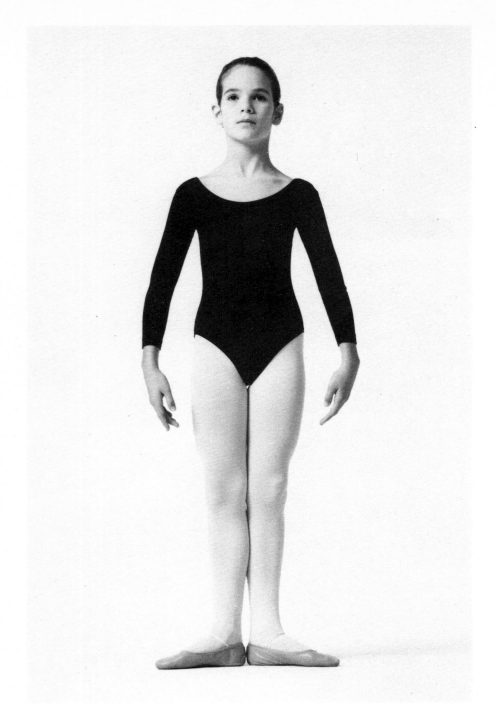

FIRST POSITION

With perfect turnout, the feet form a straight line, heels just touching each other. The arms, gently rounded, are held so that the middle finger is at the side of the thigh.

SECOND POSITION

The feet form a straight line, and depending upon leg length, the heels are about one and a half lengths of the student's foot apart. The arms, gently curved, are held palms forward, out to the sides and sloping slightly down to the fingertips. In a demi-second position, the arms are held halfway between fifth *en bas* (page 28) and second position.

THIRD POSITION

One foot is placed in front of the other with the front heel touching the middle of the back foot. One arm is held slightly curved with the little finger in front of the center of the thigh. The other arm is pulled a short distance out to the side.

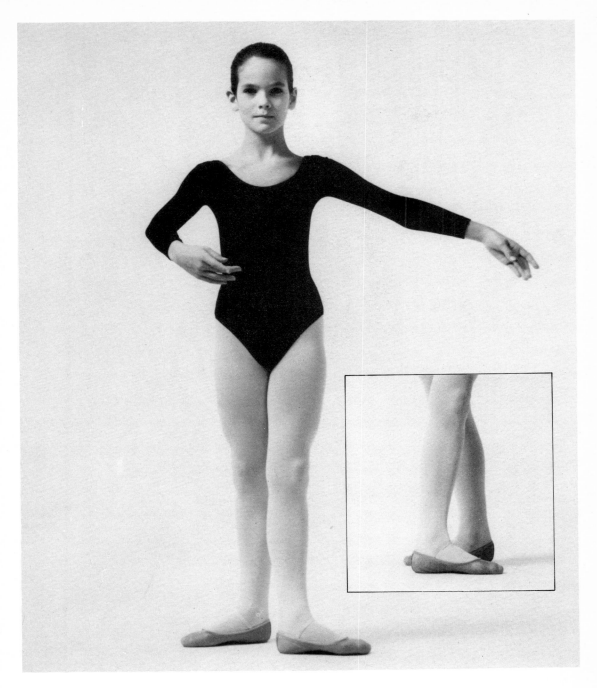

FOURTH POSITION

There are two versions of the fourth position: open and crossed feet.
In open fourth, one foot is forward from first position. The heels are
in line. In crossed fourth, one foot is forward from fifth position. The
heel of the front foot is in line with the joint of the big toe of the back
foot.

The photograph shows fourth position *en avant* (forward). One
arm is held in second position and the other arm is held gently
curved in front of the body and level with the first arm.

FIFTH POSITION

The feet are crossed, one in front of the other, so that the heel of the front foot covers the big toe joint of the back foot. Fifth position is the most difficult because it uses full turnout.

   The photograph shows fifth position *en bas* (low). The arms are held gently curved so that the fingers are in line with the center of the thigh.

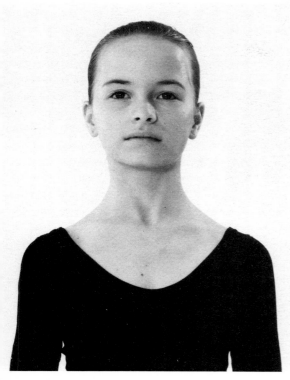

Erect.

Turned.

POSITIONS OF THE HEAD

There are five basic positions of the head: erect, turned, inclined, raised and lowered. Two positions are often combined.

Inclined.

Raised.

Lowered.

5   BEGINNER'S BARRE

The *barre* is central to ballet technique. It is used as an aid when performing exercises in preparation for work in the center of the studio. All dancers exercise at the *barre*.

When used to develop balance and strengthen the supporting leg, it should not be gripped tightly. A light grip is all that is required. However, advanced students pull hard against it when performing stretching and strengthening exercises.

DEMI-PLIÉ (Half-Bend)

A *demi-plié* is a half-bend at the knees in any one of the five positions of the feet. The legs must be well turned out from the hips and the knees in the same line as the feet. The weight of the body is evenly distributed over both feet. The heels remain firmly on the floor in all positions. This exercise helps to achieve turnout and lengthens the leg muscles.

Tendu to fourth *devant*.

Tendu to second.

BATTEMENT TENDU (Stretched Beating)

A *battement tendu* is a stretching action of the leg, ankle joint and foot. The foot is in the *pointe tendue* position, which forces the instep well outward, developing strength and helping to give a pleasing line to the leg.

The photographs show three different *tendu* exercises: *tendu* to fourth *devant* (in front), *tendu* to second, and *tendu* to fourth *derrière* (behind).

endu to fourth *derrière*.

BATTEMENT DÉGAGÉ (Disengaged Beating)

The *dégagé* is next in progression to the *tendu* but is performed at a quicker speed, with the extension controlled so that the toe stops about two inches above the floor. This exercise is used to improve speed and controlled use of the floor.

BATTEMENT FRAPPÉ (Struck Beating)

The working foot "beats" the supporting leg, then with a strong movement, the foot is thrust into second position, striking and brushing the ball of the foot along the floor and extending so that it lifts from the floor in a strong point. The foot is returned to the supporting leg without touching the floor. This exercise develops speed in stretching the leg. It prepares the student for small jumps and point work.

From first position, the foot moves to fourth *devant*.

ROND DE JAMBE À TERRE
(Round of the Leg on the Ground)

This is a circular motion performed with the leg. The foot passes from first position to fourth position *devant*, reaching outward to second position, continuing to fourth *derrière* and moving forward to pass through first position again.

In this exercise, the circular motion can be *en dehors* (outward) or *en dedans* (inward). When performed *en dehors*, the working leg circles from the front to the back; when performed *en dedans*, the working leg rotates from the back to the front. The *rond de jambe* rotates the leg in the hip.

The body is held steady as the leg moves in the hip.

The foot is returned smoothly to complete the exercise.

The arm moves out to steady the body.

GRAND BATTEMENT (Large Beating)

Beginning with straight legs, the working leg is kicked into the air, passing through the *pointe tendue* and *dégagé* positions, and then brought down slowly through the same positions. The accent is on the upward motion. Both knees are kept straight. This exercise can be performed from the front, side and back. It loosens the leg in the hip and is a preparation for many large jumps.

The working leg passes through the *pointe tendue* and *dégagé* positions.

The working leg at its maximum height.

The *retiré* is started from fifth position.

RETIRÉ (Withdrawn or Retired)

As the thigh is raised to the second position in the air, the toe is drawn up the supporting leg to come in line with the knee. The *retiré* exercise helps the student perform an important position of the foot and leg, which is used in more advanced exercises.

As the thigh comes to second position, the arm is raised to complete the movement.

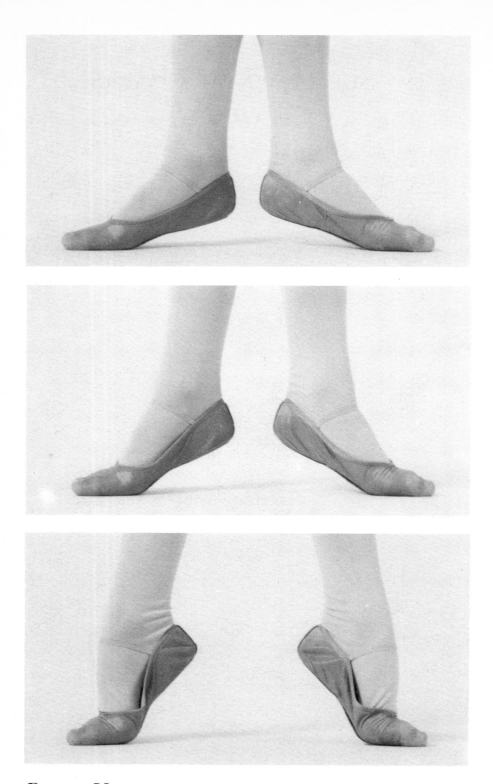

Press-Up

The body is lifted by raising the heels from the floor through ¼ , ½ , and ¾ point. The ball of the foot remains on the floor. This exercise stretches and strengthens the ankle and leg, and develops balance.

6 SUPPLEMENTARY BARRE

The positions used in more advanced *barre* exercises require greater skills. By this stage in training, the student will have developed the extra turnout, strength, speed and understanding necessary for these exercises.

GRAND PLIÉ (Large Bend)

Grand pliés are performed in all five positions. The heels are allowed to rise from the floor only as much as necessary to obtain the depth of a full *plié*, except in second and open fourth when the heels are held firmly to the floor. This exercise develops turnout and elastic muscles.

Starting position.

FONDU (Sinking Down)

In a *fondu*, the body is lowered by bending the knee of the supporting leg while the working leg comes into *cou-de-pied* (at the ankle). The working leg extends from *cou-de-pied* to a position in the air. The stretching of the supporting leg is done at the same time as the extension and lifting of the working leg. The *fondu* exercise develops strength and coordination.

The variation shown in the photograph is *fondu derrière*.

The supporting leg is stretched while the working leg is lifted.

Starting position.

PETIT BATTEMENT (Small Beating)

The heel of the working foot in *cou-de-pied* crosses in front and behind the supporting ankle with a quick sideways movement. The leg is held in second position, and the movement is from the working knee down. This exercise educates the feet to pass each other sideways and is a preparation for small beats in the air.

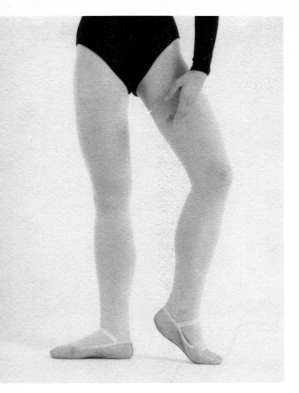

The foot moves out and is then returned behind the supporting ankle.

The foot moves out again and is returned in front of the supporting ankle.

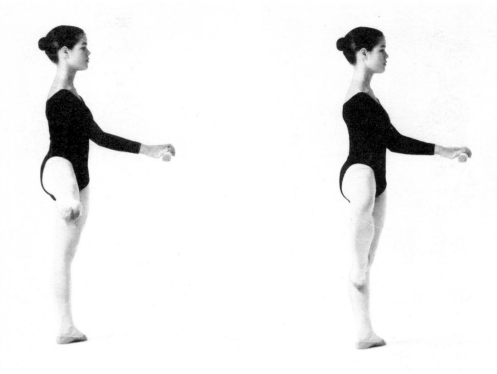

From starting position at second position in the air, the working leg is bent at the knee.

ROND DE JAMBE EN L'AIR
(Round of the Leg in the Air)

With the leg raised in second position, the working foot makes a teardrop shape in the air coming to the side of the supporting leg and back out to second position. The hips and thighs do not move. This exercise improves flexibility of the knee and control of the thigh.

In this exercise, the rotation can be *en dehors* (outward) or *en dedans* (inward). When performed *en dedans*, the working foot circles from the front to the back; when performed *en dehors,* the working foot circles from the back to the front.

The working foot traces an oval and is returned to starting
position.

From starting position, the thigh is raised to working height.

DÉVELOPPÉ (Developed or Unfolded)

The working leg is slowly unfolded from the supporting leg to an extended position in the air. This exercise helps to develop strength, create correct lines and improve balance. A *développé* can be done to the front, side and back.

The leg is slowly extended and held.

Starting position.

GRAND ROND DE JAMBE EN L'AIR
(Large Round of the Leg in the Air)

The leg is carried in the air from one fourth position, past second to the opposite fourth, making a half circle in the air. This exercise is a strong rotation of the leg and improves balance and control.

In this exercise, the rotation can be *en dehors* or *en dedans*. When performed *en dehors*, the working leg makes a half circle from the front to the back; when performed *en dedans*, the working leg makes a half circle from the back to the front.

The leg is drawn up the thigh and fully extended to the front.

In a continuous movement, the leg is carried through second position in the air.

The movement continues until the leg is behind the body.

Forward bend with one extended leg.

STRETCHES

It is important that a dancer's body be flexible. Each day's *barre* exercises end with stretches, which bend the body slowly to the front, side and back. The legs do not move. Each of these stretches can be performed with both legs straight or as shown here with one leg extended.

Side bend with one extended leg.   Back bend with one extended leg.

7 THE CENTER

A fter completing the *barre* exercises, the body is prepared to work in the center of the studio without support. Any exercise performed at the *barre* may be done in the center.

DIRECTION

Ballet is a performing art, and the students' classroom is their stage. All work in the studio is performed facing the front of the room, which is considered to be the audience. There are three basic directions of the body that present the most attractive lines to the audience.

The three basic directions are *croisé* (crossed), *en face* (facing front), and *effacé* (effaced or turned slightly from the audience). The photographs illustrate directions of the body in fifth position.

CROISÉ

The body faces diagonally to the front with the foot nearest the audience at the front.

EN FACE

The body faces the audience squarely.

EFFACÉ

The body faces diagonally to the front with the foot nearest the audience at the back.

POSITIONS OF THE BODY

The positions of the legs, arms and head and the directions of the body are combined in eight basic positions of the body.

In classical ballet movement, dancers pass through these positions. In early training, the student learns three basic positions of the body from which the others are derived. The three basic positions are leg in front, leg at the side and leg behind the body.

À LA QUATRIÈME DEVANT
(To the Fourth Front)

The direction of the body is *en face* with the leg in fourth *devant*.
Arms are in second position.

À LA SECONDE (To the Second)

The direction of the body is *en face*, with the leg and arms in the second position.

À LA QUATRIÈME DERRIÈRE
(To the Fourth Behind)

The direction of the body is *en face*, with the leg in fourth *derrière* and the arms in second position.

The following eight basic positions are the building blocks of the classical dancer's dance vocabulary.

QUATRIÈME CROISÉ DEVANT
(Fourth Crossed in Front)

The direction of the body is *croisé*. The front leg is in fourth. The raised arm is in fifth *en haut* and the side arm is in demi-second. The head is turned and inclined to the front.

QUATRIÈME DEVANT (Fourth in Front)

The direction of the body is *en face*. The front leg is in fourth, the arms are in second, and the head is erect.

ÉCARTÉ (Wide Apart)

The direction of the body is diagonally to the front. The leg is in second position. The raised arm is pulled open from fifth *en haut* and the side arm is in demi-second. The head is turned and lifted slightly to the raised arm.

Quatrième Effacé Devant
(Fourth Effaced to the Front)

The direction of the body is *effacé*, with the leg in fourth *devant*. The raised arm is in fifth *en haut* and the side arm is in demi-second. The head is inclined and turned to the front. The shoulders are pulled back to present a clear and open line of the chest.

À LA SECONDE (To the Second)

The direction of the body is *en face*. The leg is in second, the arms are in second, and the head is erect.

ÉPAULÉ (Shouldered)

The direction of the body is *effacé*. The leg is in fourth *derrière*. The arm nearest the audience is extended in front of the body and the other arm is pulled back. The shoulders are turned to expose the top of the back to the audience. The head is inclined over the front arm and turned slightly to the front.

QUATRIÈME DERRIÈRE (Fourth Behind)

The direction of the body is *en face*. The leg is in fourth *derrière*, the arms are in second position, and the head is erect.

Quatrième Croisé Derrière
(Fourth Crossed Behind)

The direction of the body is *croisé*. The back leg is in fourth *derrière*.
The raised arm is in fifth *en haut* and the side arm is in demi-second.
The head is inclined to the back leg and turned to the front.

ARABESQUE

Arabesque is a word that refers to a line in music or dance. In ballet it is a position in which the body may be in profile, on one leg; the other leg is stretched straight back and the arms are held forward to create a long and visually pleasing line. The variations are almost endless. Because the fourth and fifth *arabesques* are performed on a *demi-plié*, the foot of the supporting leg is flat. However, the first, second and third *arabesques* may be performed on flat, demi or full point. The photographs show the five basic Cecchetti *arabesques*.

FIRST ARABESQUE

The same arm is held forward as the supporting leg. The other arm is pulled back from the shoulder.

SECOND ARABESQUE

The same arm as the raised leg is held forward. The other arm is pulled back from the shoulder.

THIRD ARABESQUE

Both arms are held forward.

FOURTH ARABESQUE

When second *arabesque* is performed on a *demi-plié* in the *croisé* position, it is called fourth *arabesque*.

FIFTH ARABESQUE

When third *arabesque* is performed on a *demi-plié* in a *croisé*
position, it is called fifth *arabesque*.

ATTITUDE

The *attitude* position in ballet comes from the statue of Mercury by Giovanni da Bologna. *Attitudes* may be performed in a *devant* or *derrière* position. In the Cecchetti *attitude*, one leg is lifted with the knee bent and turned out so that it is higher than the foot.

Generally, in *attitude derrière*, the same arm as leg is raised. In the *devant* position, the opposite arm is raised. Although either arm may be used, the four photographs that follow illustrate the basic *attitudes*.

ATTITUDE CROISÉE DERRIÈRE
(Crossed Behind)

An *attitude derrière* with the body in a *croisé* position. The raised arm is in fifth *en haut* and the opposite arm in second position. The head is erect and turned to the front.

CECCHETTI ATTITUDE CROISÉE DERRIÈRE

In this example of a Cecchetti *attitude*, the body is in *croisé* position. The same arm as raised leg is lifted to *écarté* position and pulled in front of the shoulder instead of being held at the side. The opposite arm is in a low *arabesque.* The head is erect and slightly lifted to the raised arm.

ATTITUDE EFFACÉE DERRIÈRE
(Effaced Behind)

An *attitude derrière* done with the arms, head and body in *effacé* position.

ATTITUDE CROISÉE DEVANT
(Crossed in Front)

Generally done in *croisé* position, the leg is raised in front and the arms and head are in fourth *croisé devant* position. In the *devant* position, the raised leg is more stretched or open than in the *attitude derrière*.

RELEVÉ (Raised)

The extension of press-ups (page 44) are *relevés*. A *relevé* is a light, quick lift of the body from a small *plié* with the foot in a perfect line with the leg. This is an important exercise in preparation for point work.

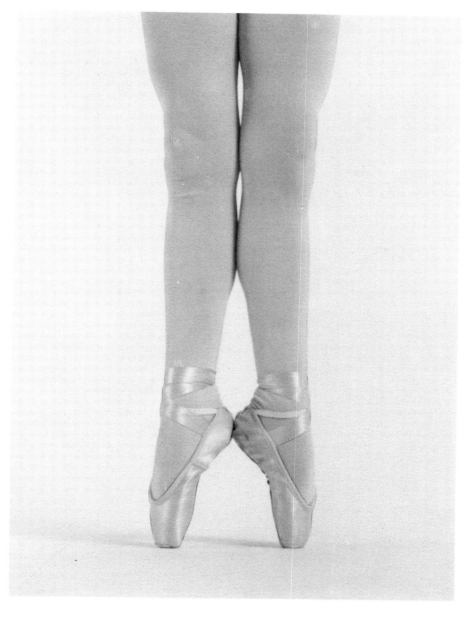

RELEVÉ IN FIRST POSITION

The toes are under the instep and straight, with the heels together.

RELEVÉ IN FIFTH POSITION

As in fifth position *à terre*, the feet are together with the back foot almost hidden.

RELEVÉ IN SECOND

The legs and feet are in second position.

SUR LA POINTE (On Point)

In ballet, unlike in any other form of dance, the female dancer rises to the ends of her toes. This position is known as being "on point."

In addition to offering the audience a pleasing long line of the leg, the dancer on point looks light and delicate.

A student should not try point work before she is ready. Point work requires careful preparation through training to sufficiently strengthen ankles, insteps, legs, and stomach and seat muscles.

A more advanced form of *relevé* is from two feet to one foot. The example shown is *relevé devant* or a slight spring from two feet to one foot. The working foot is drawn quickly up in front of the supporting leg.

8 ADVANCED CENTER WORK

Starting position.

PIROUETTE (Spin)

A *pirouette* is a spin on one leg done in any position. The simple *pirouette* performed in the early years of training is usually done from fifth position. The photographs show a *pirouette* position in which the arms are held in a low fifth position *en avant* and are then drawn closer to the body. The leg remains in *relevé devant*.

The *pirouette*, or any turn, can be performed *en dehors* (turning outward, away from the supporting leg) or *en dedans* (turning inward, toward the supporting leg).

This example shows a *pirouette* from fifth to fifth *en dehors*.

In a turn, the head remains facing front while the body begins to turn, and then is quickly brought around to the front followed by the body. This prevents dizziness and keeps the dancer from losing his or her sense of direction.

ADAGE/ADAGIO (At Ease)

The ability to hold positions and move from position to position with control is developed in *adage*, an important part of every ballet class. *Adage* is a series of slowly moving exercises, which develop lyricism, quality of line, strength, and balance through controlled movement.

The photograph shows the student in a *fondu* with the working foot in *cou-de-pied*.

ALLÉGRO (Brisk Movement)

Allégro is a series of small and large jumps and large moving steps.
Allégro, which teaches a student the timing of more rapid
movements, is the climax of a ballet class.

   As in all sections of the class, the movements that come before the
allégro are designed to prepare the student for this work. The ability
to connect jumping steps smoothly is difficult to master; therefore,
the *allégro* always begins with simple, connected small jumps.

   The jump in the photograph is called a *soubresaut*, a spring into
the air in fifth position.

PAS DE DEUX (Dance for Two)

The partnering of boys and girls brings something entirely new into the student's experience. Learning to move with and trust a partner takes a little extra effort.

Partnering, or *pas de deux*, is one of the later developments of training. The *adage*, or *adagio*, is an important part of *pas de deux*. It is in the *adage* that ballerinas perform *arabesques, développés*, supported turns and other movements that will show a slowly moving, graceful line.

Like the *barre*, the male dancer supports the ballerina as she slowly performs the most graceful positions. Later on in the *pas de deux*, the male dancer will have his chance to perform the high jumps and the strong athletic movements associated with his role, but the *adage* belongs to his partner.

9 MAKING A BALLET

People are always coming up with new ideas, and people in ballet are no exception. Often the idea may be for a brand-new ballet, but sometimes it will be a new idea for an old favorite.

All ballets change over time. Even the Romantic ballets of the mid-1800s and Tchaikovsky's Classical ballets change, not only from the originals, but also from year to year.

As time passes, audiences have different ideas about what they like. More importantly, so do choreographers. What may have been exciting at one time can become boring and need a breath of new life. Or a ballet company may have a new dancer who can leap or turn very well. Then the choreographer may change a ballet to show the dancer's special talents.

In changing old ballets or making new ones, choreographers are very important. It is their job to come up with the new ideas. They decide what movements and music will be used, who will dance what part, and even what the costumes, sets and lights will be like. Although sets, costumes and lights are the jobs of special designers, the choreographer approves their work.

When the choreographer has an idea for a new ballet, he or she discusses it with a composer, or if existing music is being used, the ballet company's conductor.

Many things now happen at the same time. The conductor starts introducing the arrangement of the music to the orchestra. Just like the choreography, the music can be played in different ways.

The choreographer begins work with the dancers. The ballet is actually created at this time. Although the choreographer has some ideas about the steps in the new ballet, a lot of help will come from the dancers in working out the steps.

The company choreologist is the person who keeps track of it all. Using a system of symbols, the choreologist writes down each movement of each dancer. There are two main systems of dance notation, both invented in this century and both named after their inventors, Rudolf Benesh and Rudolf von Laban. Orchestra members read sheets of music, which record forever the individual notes that make up the musical score. Until dance notation was invented, dancers had to remember the steps of ballets from one year to the next. Some ballets were even lost because nobody could remember them. Now, with notation, that can never happen again.

The costume and scenery designers sketch their ideas and show them to the choreographer. The costumes may be beautiful or plain. In many new ballets, the dancers wear simple leotards or body tights. The scenic designer will suggest "sets" of scenery for each act of the ballet. Like the costumes, these can range from elaborate and expensive to simple and easily built.

Lighting directors are designers, too. They decide the number, type and color of the lights that will shine on the stage. Stage lights not only allow the audience to see, but also spotlight particular dancers and help set a mood. For example, blue lights make us feel cold and might be used in a scene with witches at midnight. Red lights make us feel warm and might be used in a tender love scene. The lights keep changing all the way through the performance, following the mood of the music. The colors must be carefully chosen to go with the costumes and the scenery.

Production managers are responsible for the mechanical aspects of performing a ballet on stage, such as the operation of the lighting and sound system and the installation and removal of sets. They must make sure that everything works and that the people who will operate the stage equipment know their jobs. When a company is on tour, performing away from its home city, the production manager is in charge of setting up and then removing all of the equipment from each theater and sending it on to the next one where it will be set up again.

Until now, everyone who helps make a ballet has been working in separate groups. The dancers have practiced in a studio with a piano to accompany them, while the orchestra has rehearsed the music elsewhere. During this time, the sets have been built and painted, the lights chosen, and the costumes sewn.

We are now ready for a full rehearsal. Rehearsals continue until opening night. Several are held on stage.

There may be a placing rehearsal where the dancers are able to see and feel the size of the stage. The choreographer can then tell who should move a little in or out, forward or backward.

At a technical rehearsal, the lighting and sets are used for the first time. Until now, the dancers have imagined sets, using chairs and other things to show where a set might be.

During the technical rehearsal, the dancers will sometimes "mark" their steps. This means that they will not dance all out as they would in a performance. Instead, they will perform all of their movements and steps in a relaxed way. This rehearsal is not really held for them, but for the technical stage crew who will operate the lights and move the sets.

The entire ballet has now been performed, from start to finish, many times. Sometimes a rough dress rehearsal is held. Everything is as it will be on opening night with lights, orchestra and the full company dancing, but the dancers do not wear their costumes.

Finally, it is time for the full dress rehearsal. The dancers wear their makeup and costumes, and everyone pretends that it is opening night. The choreographer sits and watches the performance for small mistakes that would not be noticed until the costumes are worn.

American choreographer Glen Tetley rehearses Karen Kain and
Frank Augustyn for their starring roles in the ballet *Sphinx*.

Because ballet costumes cost a great deal of money, they are not worn until the last minute, in case they are damaged. The costumes may look flimsy and glamorous, but they must be very strong to withstand the hard physical punishment that they will receive from the jumping and stretching dancers.

The time spent in rehearsal has been put to good use by other people in the ballet company. The public relations staff has spread the news of the new ballet to magazines and newspapers, and has advertised the performances. Unless people know about the new ballet and want to come to see it, all of the company's work will have gone to waste.

For opening night, they have invited reporters and important people. They hope that the newspaper critics will like the ballet and will write good reviews. When people read a good review and hear about the important people who went to see the ballet on opening night, they will want to come, too.

The months of work on the new ballet are over. It is now part of the company's repertoire and will be performed many times before it, too, is changed.

10 FAMOUS BALLET STARS

As we have seen, although ballet is very popular today, it was not always popular. It usually took a particularly exciting person to bring new life into the ballet world once more. The short list that follows includes some of the important ballet people who, during their careers, have changed ballet for the better.

Marie Taglioni, born in 1804, made her début in 1822 during the Romantic period. Her father, an Italian ballet master, made her work so hard that, at times, she collapsed with exhaustion. She was one of the first dancers to go on point. When she played the lead in *La Sylphide*, dancing her father's choreography, she became a sensation. All over Europe, people wanted to see *La Sylphide* and Taglioni. Soon she was copied by other ballerinas. Even her hairstyle, parted down the middle, was copied. Marie Taglioni will be remembered forever as the Queen of Romantic Ballet.

Anna Pavlova was born in Russia in 1881. She first came to public attention as a member of the Ballets Russes, where she danced with Vaslav Nijinsky. She left the Ballets Russes to form her own company and to tour the world. Pavlova took ballet to towns and cities that had never seen it before. Her most remembered role was *The Dying Swan*. Like Taglioni before her, she is remembered for the special talent she brought to the art of dance.

Mikhail Fokine was a year older than Pavlova and, like her, a Russian. He was the choreographic genius behind the Ballets Russes. With superior dancers like the Cecchetti-trained Pavlova and Nijinsky, he created a style of ballet theater that relied on costume, scenery and acting as well as music and dance. Fokine created the highly dramatic productions that made the Ballets Russes the most exciting ballet company in the world. Among his many creations are the ballets *The Dying Swan*, *Firebird* and *Petrushka*.

Vaslav Nijinsky, another Russian, was born in 1889. He was the ideal dancer for Fokine's ballets. Before the Ballets Russes, ballet had become a pleasant evening out for audiences, offering little challenge or excitement. Nijinsky changed that. He was a great actor as well as the most gifted dancer that the stage had ever seen. He captivated his audiences. It is said that they believed he stopped in mid-air during his amazing leaps. Choreographer of several works, he is most widely known for *The Rite of Spring*. Igor Stravinsky's music and Nijinsky's choreography for this ballet were so unusual that fist fights broke out in the audience when it was first presented.

Above Rudolf Nureyev.

Left Anna Pavlova.

Mikhail Baryshnikov.

Erik Bruhn.

Vaslav Nijinsky.

Erik Bruhn, born in 1928, is the great dancer of the Danish school. He was the finest dancer of his generation and helped make the Danish style better known throughout the world. He continues to be in great demand as a choreographer and has directed the national companies of Sweden and Canada.

Rudolf Nureyev was born in 1938 in Soviet Asia. He began to study ballet at the Kirov School when he was seventeen. His fierce independence led him to defect from Russia in 1961. After his defection, he danced with Dame Margot Fonteyn and the Royal Ballet for five years. Nureyev has since appeared as a guest artist with many companies and has choreographed and produced his works on television and in theatres worldwide.

Mikhail Baryshnikov, ten years younger than Nureyev, is his successor as the most popular male dancer today. He, too, defected from the Kirov. When he joined the American Ballet Theatre, Baryshnikov was Natalia Makarova's partner. He is known as a technically perfect dancer.

There are other people who have improved ballet and made it more exciting for audiences. For example, two of the greatest choreographers in history, Sir Frederick Ashton and George Balanchine, worked in this century. Teachers such as August Bournonville, Enrico Cecchetti and Agrippina Vaganova were responsible for the superior dancing styles of their students, and their influence has been felt around the world. Because of her great experience, Dame Margot Fonteyn is the reigning senior ballerina, although she has now retired from one of the longest careers in ballet. Natalia Makarova, who lives in New York City, and Galina Samsova, who lives in London, are two of several ballerinas who have now succeeded Miss Fonteyn as ballet's greatest performers. All of these people and more have contributed a great deal to ballet, and its current popularity is due to them.

11
THE STORIES OF FAMOUS BALLETS

CINDERELLA

Music by Serge Prokofiev. First performed by the Bolshoi Ballet at the Bolshoi Theatre, Moscow, November, 1945. This version choreographed by Sir Frederick Ashton and first presented by the Sadler's Wells Ballet at Covent Garden, London, December, 1945.

ACT ONE

Cinderella, in ragged clothing, is crouching beside the huge stone fireplace in her father's house. Although she looks very tired and sad, we can see that she is a beautiful girl. Her father is sitting at a table reading, while her two nasty stepsisters are sitting by him busily sewing a scarf.

The sisters are making the scarf for a fancy dress ball to be held later that evening. Although there are two sisters, they are making only one scarf. When it is finished, they start to fight over which one will wear it to the party.

Cinderella watches them selfishly fighting. Her poor father tries to calm them down, but the two sisters ignore him as they tug and pull at the scarf. Finally, it rips in two. Her father can do nothing with these girls; they argue all of the time. They leave the room, still fighting, and he follows them, looking quite upset.

Cinderella is now alone. She picks up her broom and moves gracefully around the room with it. Her sisters have left behind the torn scarf. Picking up a piece of it, she drapes it around her shoulders and pretends that she is a fine lady, the kind of person that her own mother was. She lights a candlestick from the fire and holds it up to her mother's picture hanging above the fireplace. "How beautiful she was," thinks Cinderella.

Just then, Cinderella's father comes back into the room. Seeing his daughter, he tries to comfort her, but he, too, is sad. When the stepsisters return, they start to scold him for keeping Cinderella from her housework.

They are interrupted by an ugly old woman at the door, begging. While her stepsisters run away to the other side of the room, Cinderella gives the old woman all that she can, a piece of bread. The old woman thanks her for her kindness and leaves, much to the relief of the two sisters.

Magali Messac as Cinderella in the American Ballet Theatre
production of *Cinderella*, choreographed by Mikhail Baryshnikov
and Peter Anastos.

Soon everyone is busy with preparations for the ball. Tailors, hairdressers, jewellers and a dancing teacher help the miserable sisters get ready. The two girls love all of the attention and act very silly. When they have finished dressing, their carriage arrives and they leave for the ball.

Now Cinderella is alone, but not for long. The old woman comes back. Before Cinderella's eyes, she turns into a beautiful fairy princess. She tells Cinderella that she is really her fairy godmother and that she will help Cinderella go to the ball.

Before Cinderella can ask how, four fairies dress her in a beautiful gown. The fairy godmother waves her magic wand and turns a pumpkin into a magnificent carriage pulled by white horses. She warns Cinderella that the magic spell will disappear by midnight. At the stroke of twelve, Cinderella must be home. Promising that she will be home by then, Cinderella rides off to the ball.

ACT TWO

The ball has already started, and we join it as the two wicked sisters arrive. Many of the guests are dancing. The two sisters also try to dance, but people laugh at them because they are such bad dancers.

The Prince comes in and is greeted by his guests. The two sisters try to catch his attention, but he ignores them. At last, Cinderella's coach arrives. The Prince goes to see who has such a magnificent carriage. Cinderella is helped out, and the Prince falls in love with her beauty at once.

Holding her arm, he takes her for a walk in the palace garden, while his guests start to dance once more. When the couple returns to the ball, the Prince dances alone. Then it is Cinderella's turn, and she dances a graceful solo full of joy. Finally, they join in a *pas de deux*, which ends with the Prince kneeling before her while Cinderella *pirouettes*.

They are obviously in love. A page brings an orange on a silver tray. The orange is the most prized treasure in the whole kingdom. The Prince gives it to Cinderella as a sign of his love. He also gives oranges to the two sisters, who immediately begin to fight about which one has the larger orange.

Now the Prince and Cinderella lead the court in a bright, romantic dance, and the guests are caught up in the magic of the evening. As the dance continues, the cymbals begin to shimmer and we hear a clock ticking loudly. It is almost midnight! Cinderella is panic-stricken. She does not want to leave the Prince, but she must if she is not to be found out. The cymbals crash. This is Cinderella's final warning, and she tears herself away from the poor Prince, who does not understand what is happening.

She runs through the palace as fast as she can, and by the time she arrives at the gate, she is in rags. Her dream night is over. Her beautiful gown and carriage have disappeared. She is ragged Cinderella once more. The orchestra plays the theme for the *pas de deux* and the curtain falls.

Robert LaFosse and Victor Barbee as the wicked stepsisters in the American Ballet Theatre production.

ACT THREE

We find Cinderella by the fire again. The warm fire has made her sleepy, and she is unsure if she dreamt about the ball or if it really did happen.

When she finds a glass slipper in the pocket of her apron, she knows that it must have been true. She is so happy that she begins to dance, pretending her broom is the Prince.

Interrupted by her returning sisters, she listens as they tell tales about themselves and the Prince, showing their oranges to try to prove their stories. Cinderella doesn't care; she knows what really happened.

The sisters start to take off their uncomfortable gowns when a great commotion is heard in the street. The Prince is coming! He is looking for the beautiful girl from the ball. When she is found, he wants to marry her. The sisters quickly dress and are all smiles as the Prince enters their house.

He holds a glass slipper that was left behind by his lost love. The girl whose foot fits the slipper will be his bride. Not even noticing Cinderella in her rags, he asks the wicked stepsisters to try on the slipper.

The first one tries and can get only her toes into the dainty shoe. The second sister has such a hard time that Cinderella comes to help her. As she bends down, the other glass slipper falls from her apron. The surprised Prince insists that she, too, try on the slipper. Her stepsisters protest, but he ignores them.

Cinderella puts on the shoe and it fits perfectly. The Prince announces that Cinderella will be his bride. The sisters start to argue, but when they see that it will do no good, they ask Cinderella for forgiveness. Cinderella is a kind girl and forgives them.

ACT THREE – SCENE TWO

We find ourselves in a magical garden with sparkling lights. A large boat is waiting to take the Prince and Cinderella away. The Prince's friends are dancing with the fairies when he and Cinderella enter.

The music repeats the theme of love first heard when the lovers met at the ball. The fairy godmother, fairies and the Prince's friends wish them well as they board the boat and sail away to happiness forever.

GISELLE

Music by Adolphe Adam. Story by Vernoy de Saint-Georges, Théophile Gautier and Jean Coralli. Choreography by Jules Perrot and Jean Coralli. First performed at the Théâtre de l'Académie Royale de Musique, Paris, June, 1841.

Giselle was produced in the great Romantic period, when stories of fairies, nymphs and other supernatural creatures were very popular. One of the legends that Romantic poets loved was the story of young women called Wilis. Wilis were girls who had been engaged to be married and who died before their wedding days. They appeared at night and danced by moonlight in their bridal dresses. Angry at their own deaths, they would trap young men and make them dance with them until they died, too.

ACT ONE

The orchestra plays an overture, and the curtain rises to show a village on the Rhine River in Germany.

In the village we see peasant girls and boys talking and laughing. The cottage of Giselle and her mother is in the background. Outside their cottage stands Hilarion, the gamekeeper, who is in love with Giselle. He quickly hides when he sees two men going up to Giselle's door. It is Albrecht, Duke of Silesia and his attendant, Wilfrid. Albrecht is disguised as a peasant. Before he knocks on the door, he gives his Duke's cloak and sword to Wilfrid and tells him to hide them from Giselle.

Albrecht knocks on the cottage door and then hides. Giselle opens the door and looks around outside, wondering who it could have been. Finally, Albrecht shows himself and admits he has been teasing her.

The two lovers dance outside the cottage and then sit on a bench. Giselle picks a wild flower and plays "he loves me, he loves me not" with the petals. They are obviously very much in love and, linking arms, they start to dance again.

Hilarion has been watching them from his hiding place. He is so jealous that he runs out and pushes Albrecht away. Falling on his knees, Hilarion tells Giselle that it is he who is her true love, not Albrecht. Giselle is very angry with Hilarion. She makes fun of him

Veronica Tennant as Giselle with Hazaros Surmeyan as Hilarion
and Frank Augustyn as Albrecht in The National Ballet of Canada
production of *Giselle*.

and tells him to go away. Before Hilarion leaves, he shakes his fist at Albrecht.

Giselle's friends, the village girls, now enter the scene and start to dance. Albrecht is joined by the village boys and he, Giselle and all of their friends dance with great happiness.

Giselle's mother, Berthe, hears the dancing and comes out to warn Giselle that if she dances too much she will die and become a Wili. Taking her daughter by the hand, she leads Giselle home, leaving Albrecht to wander off alone.

The stage is empty as Hilarion sneaks back. Suddenly, a hunting horn sounds and he runs to hide. A hunting party appears. It is the Prince of Courland and his daughter, Bathilde, with huntsmen and court followers.

They stop at Giselle's cottage and ask for something to drink. Giselle brings out wine for them and then sits at the Princess's feet. Feeling the fabric of Bathilde's gown, she tells her how beautiful the dress looks on her. The Princess asks Giselle what she loves the most. Giselle answers that, above all, she loves to dance and, getting up, shows the Princess a few quick steps.

The Princess is delighted and rewards Giselle by taking off her own necklace and giving it to her. The hunting party now goes into Giselle's cottage. The Prince leaves his hunting horn outside and tells his hunters that a call on his horn will signal them to return.

This is Hilarion's chance! He has decided to tell Giselle that Albrecht is a Duke and not the ordinary man that he is pretending to be. He waits until Albrecht and the village boys and girls return and Giselle comes out to dance with them once more.

While they are dancing, Hilarion comes out of hiding and tells Giselle who Albrecht really is. He asks her if she can ever trust a man who has lied to her. Poor Albrecht. He is afraid that he will lose Giselle's love, but he has to admit it is all true.

Furious at the gamekeeper for trying to separate him from Giselle's love, Albrecht grabs his sword and tries to kill Hilarion, but Wilfrid stops him. The sword drops to the ground.

Hilarion is now very happy, not noticing that he has made Giselle sad. He blows the hunter's horn to call the hunting party. When they hear the horn, the Prince and his daughter rush out of the cottage to see what is happening. Bathilde asks Albrecht why he, a Duke, is dressed in peasant's clothes. Albrecht kneels and kisses her hand. Giselle is jealous. The Princess points to the engagement ring on her finger. She is the fiancée of Albrecht, Duke of Silesia.

Giselle's heart is broken, and she tears the necklace the Princess has just given her from her neck. Her mother tries to make her feel better, but it is no use. Giselle falls to the ground overcome by her sadness.

Standing around her, the village boys and girls and the hunting party feel sorry for her. She seems so helpless. Giselle rises and slowly acts out the happy dance that she and Albrecht had performed. She holds an imaginary flower and picks the petals in a pretend "he loves me, he loves me not."

Picking up Albrecht's sword, she dances, dragging it along the ground. Suddenly she raises it and plunges it into her heart. Now, dying, she dances the dance of love that she had performed with Albrecht. Running to her mother, she collapses. Albrecht holds her and as she touches his face, she dies.

Albrecht is enraged at Hilarion and again tries to kill him. Once more, Wilfrid stops him. The sad villagers move away, leaving Albrecht with Giselle.

ACT TWO

The curtain rises on a misty forest at midnight. A small lake is seen in the moonlight and Giselle's grave, marked by a large cross, is by the lake.

Hunters come and sit by the lake. Hilarion joins them. They are all frightened by the moonlit woods and talk of the Wilis that may be about. Hilarion would like to visit Giselle's grave but follows the others when they begin to leave.

Myrtha, Queen of the Wilis, appears at the back of the stage wearing a veil and a long white dress. She poses in *arabesque* and then begins a dance to call the Wilis. When they appear, they dance to her command as she dances around and in between them.

Ordering them to stop, she leads them to Giselle's grave. Touching the grave with a magic branch, she watches the earth part and Giselle rise from the grave. Giselle is dressed in white and wears a veil, which Myrtha removes.

She seems hypnotized as she follows Myrtha in a dance that will make her a Wili. Myrtha tells her that she is now one of them and orders her to dance alone. Giselle comes to life, rejoicing in her freedom from the grave. She leaves the stage after her dance, while Myrtha orders the other Wilis to hide.

Albrecht walks slowly onto the empty stage. He has come to visit Giselle's grave as a sign of his undying love. Giselle appears, teases and then dances with him. Using her magic, she keeps disappearing and then coming back to dance with the joyful Albrecht. Finally, she leaves and Albrecht follows her into the forest.

Hilarion enters the stage and is trapped by Myrtha and her Wilis. He pleads to be let go, but Myrtha orders them to throw him into the lake. The hypnotized Wilis do as they are told and Hilarion is drowned. Myrtha leads the Wilis away.

The unsuspecting Albrecht returns and is also trapped by Myrtha. He begs for his life, but Myrtha says no. He, too, must die. Giselle pleads for him, but it is no use. She tells Albrecht to run to her grave and to hold the cross, then the Wilis cannot harm him.

He reaches the grave before the Wilis. Myrtha is furious. She does not like to be disobeyed. Giselle stands in front of him to protect him, but when Myrtha orders her to dance, she cannot refuse. She dances alone amongst the standing Wilis. Albrecht leaves the protection of the cross and, with Giselle, goes down the line of Wilis pleading for their help. They all refuse. Giselle and Albrecht begin a *pas de deux*. The Willis try to come between them, but their love is so strong that they cannot be separated.

Myrtha commands Giselle to dance alone. A series of solos for Albrecht follow. Myrtha knows that he will keep dancing as long as Giselle does, but Giselle is a Wili and can dance forever. Albrecht will dance to his death.

After another variation, Albrecht is very tired and pleads to dance no more. But it is no use; dance he must. Exhausted and falling, he dances with Giselle, who pities her love but cannot help.

Four o'clock sounds. It is almost dawn, and the Wilis must return to their graves. Albrecht is saved! Giselle must also return and, as the other Wilis rush to their graves, she is both sad and happy.

Albrecht throws himself on the ground of Giselle's now closed grave. He knows that they will never see each other again.

Frank Augustyn as Albrecht, Karen Kain as Giselle and Nadia Potts
as the Queen of the Wilis in The National Ballet of Canada
production.

The Nutcracker

Music by Peter Ilyich Tchaikovsky. Story by Lev Ivanov. First performed at the Maryinsky Theatre, St. Petersburg, December, 1892.

Act One

The curtain rises to reveal the inside of a large house. This is the home of Dr. and Mrs. Stahlbaum and their children, Marie and Fritz. (Marie is called Clara in most versions of *The Nutcracker*.)

It is Christmas Eve and there is going to be a party. Through the keyhole in the door, the two children have been watching their parents and the maid decorate the huge room. Now Marie and Fritz are lying in the hallway, fast asleep.

They are awakened by the noise of family friends and their children arriving for the Christmas party. The doors are opened and the children enter the room, gazing at the tree and the wrapped presents with great excitement.

Refreshments are served, and then it is time to open the presents. The children are sitting quietly looking at their presents, when the lights go on and off. We see an old man standing at the door. He is Herr Drosselmeyer, a family friend and Marie's godfather. He is an unusual old man, who makes moving toys. With him are his nephew and three huge boxes, which contain a Harlequin doll, a Columbine doll and a toy soldier.

The huge toys dance to merry tunes, and everyone is delighted with them. When the old man brings out a large toy soldier (the Nutcracker) and gives it to Marie, Fritz becomes very jealous and jumps on it. Drosselmeyer's nephew chases Fritz away, while the old man tries to fix the Nutcracker.

Marie and the other girls go off to play with their dolls quietly, but the noisy boys try to spoil their fun by marching past with loud drums and bugles. The nephew brings Marie a bed for the Nutcracker. She tucks him in and puts him under the tree. Dr. and Mrs. Stahlbaum lead the guests in one last dance before the children have to go to bed. When they have finished, the children say good night and leave the room.

It is now midnight. The large room is dark and empty. Marie creeps in and, hugging the Nutcracker, carries him off to a quiet corner

Drosselmeyer gives the Nutcracker doll to Marie in the New York
City Ballet production of *The Nutcracker*.

where she lies down and falls asleep. While she is asleep, the old man sneaks in and finishes fixing the Nutcracker. When he is finished, he sneaks out, leaving the Nutcracker in Marie's arms.

Marie is awakened by the lights flashing on and off. A big rat comes into the room and, although Marie is very frightened, she manages to hide. The Christmas tree, the toy soldiers and the rest of the toys begin to grow bigger. The house mice grow, too. A battle is fought between the mice and the soldiers. The mice are winning until the Nutcracker arrives to lead the army against the King of the Mice.

The Nutcracker orders cannon, loaded with candy, to be fired at the mice. During the battle, Marie throws her slipper at the mouse king, and the Nutcracker stabs him with his sword. The mice run away when they see their dead king, and the battle is won.

When the tired Marie falls onto her bed, it immediately rises up and flies like a magic carpet. It takes her to the Kingdom of Snow. There waiting for her is the Nutcracker, now a handsome prince. He gives her the crown that was captured from the mouse king.

ACT TWO

The curtain rises and we see the Land of Sweets, a kingdom ruled by the Sugarplum Fairy. The Sugarplum Fairy and her angels dance to the famous "Dance of the Sugarplum Fairy" theme. The fairy then welcomes different kinds of candy – chocolates, candy boxes and marzipans – as they appear before her.

The music announces the arrival of Marie and the Nutcracker Prince. He introduces Marie to the Sugarplum Fairy. They give a pantomime of the battle with the King of the Mice, and the fairy is delighted.

She seats them on thrones, and they watch the subjects of the Land of Sweets perform a dance. When it is finished, the Sugarplum Fairy and her knight perform a *pas de deux* for Marie and the Nutcracker Prince. Marie loves the dance. She wants to dance just like the Sugarplum Fairy when she grows up.

The candies return as the Sugarplum Fairy and her knight watch Marie and the Nutcracker step into a reindeer-drawn sleigh. They wave as Marie and the Nutcracker Prince are carried away into the sky.

The Kingdom of Snow scene from the New York City Ballet production.

La Sylphide

Music by Jean Schneitzhoeffer. Story by Adolphe Nourrit. Choreography by Filippo Taglioni. First performed at the Théâtre de l'Académie Royale de Musique, Paris, March, 1832.

Act One

We see a large room in a Scottish farmhouse. James, the young man who lives in the house, is asleep in a chair. Today is his wedding day, and he is dressed in his best kilt.

James is restless in his sleep. A sylph, a fairy-like creature, is sitting at his feet. She is gazing longingly at James. Gurn, a young friend, is asleep by the fireplace. His sleep is not disturbed by the sylph, because he dreams of Effie, James's bride-to-be. Gurn is in love with Effie.

The sylph floats around James, and when he awakes with a start, he sees her. But when he reaches out for her, she vanishes. Gurn now wakes up, but he knows nothing of the sylph. He has been lost in his dream.

Effie and James's mother enter the room, and James kisses his fiancée's hand. The jealous Gurn tries to kiss her as well, but Effie pulls her hand away. Now the bridesmaids enter and give Effie her wedding gifts. Gurn asks them if they will speak to Effie about his love for her, but they refuse.

While everyone is busy talking, James goes to the fireplace and looks at the spot where the sylph disappeared. Only Gurn notices James's unusual behaviour. From a dark corner of the room comes Old Madge, the village witch. Everyone is glad to see her, and they ask her to tell their fortunes. James, however, is angry and wants her to leave.

No wonder! When she tells Effie's fortune, Old Madge tells her that James does not love her. Old Madge is sent away, and James is relieved when Effie says that she does not believe the old witch. James's mother tells everyone that it is time to go. James is troubled at the thought of being alone, but wishes them well.

Except for Gurn, sulking in the corner, James is alone. The sylph reappears and tells James that she loves him. Poor James is very confused. The sylph tells him that she will die if he marries Effie. He admits that he loves her more than Effie. She is delighted, and picking up Effie's plaid marriage shawl, she puts it on and poses as the bride. James can resist no longer and kisses her.

All this time, Gurn has been watching. He hurries upstairs to tell Effie about James and the sylph. Effie and the wedding party come rushing down to see for themselves, but the sylph has disappeared. They accuse Gurn of spreading jealous gossip, and he leaves the room sulking.

James's mother and her friends join the rest of the wedding party, and soon everyone except James is dancing. Effie asks him to dance with her, and as they dance, the sylph returns. This time, only James can see her, and the *pas de deux* with Effie becomes a *pas de trois* as the sylph imitates Effie's movements. When the guests join in, the sylph darts to and fro among them, teasing James.

Frank Augustyn as James and Nadia Potts as the sylph in The National Ballet of Canada production of *La Sylphide*.

The wedding ceremony is about to begin. Everyone quickly takes their places while James and Effie stand side by side. When it is time to exchange rings, the sylph, invisible to all but James, returns and steals Effie's ring just as James is putting it on her finger!

The guests are shocked and James is very confused. Turning to the sylph, he listens as she tells him again that she will die if he marries Effie. James believes her and the sylph makes him disappear, too. The guests are in an uproar and Effie is in tears. Where is the bridegroom?

The guests gather around Effie, who is sitting by the fire. Her plaid shawl is placed around her shoulders and the wedding veil is removed. Gurn sits at her feet.

ACT TWO

It is night. Old Madge is standing in a cave in the woods. A large pot hangs over a fire, and she is performing her witchcraft. After she is joined by other witches, Old Madge plucks a shimmering scarf out of the pot. When the other witches try to grab the magic scarf, she holds it tightly and orders them to go away.

As the sun rises, we see the trees outside the cave. James enters the woods wearing white, the costume of a sylph bridegroom. The sylph appears. When James offers her a bird's nest as a gift, she refuses and puts it back in the tree.

Calling a band of sylphs to surround them, she teases James by disappearing every time he tries to hold her. Another sylph magically appears in her place each time. James is upset. As the sun rises higher in the sky, the sylphs vanish.

James is now alone and unhappy. Why does the sylph tease him? He understood it when they were in his house, but now that he has said he loves her, why does she hide? Old Madge enters and asks what he is doing. Telling her the story of the sylph and his wedding day, he begs Old Madge to help him. Holding out the magic scarf, she tells James to throw it around the sylph. Once covered, the sylph will lose her wings and will not be able to fly. She will have to stay with him forever.

Old Madge leaves and the sylph appears. James gives her the magic scarf and she is delighted with the gift. But as soon as the scarf is around her shoulders, her wings fall off and she clutches her heart.

She stumbles and pushes James away as he tries to help. Suddenly, she dies. James kneels beside her, crying. As Old Madge laughs in the distance, the sylph's fairy sisters come and tenderly lift her up and take her away.

James is in anguish. Across the fields, he sees a wedding procession. It is Gurn and Effie and their wedding party. The joy that could have been his is now Gurn's.

Veronica Tennant as the sylph and Frank Augustyn as James in
The National Ballet of Canada production.

Swan Lake

Music by Peter Ilyich Tchaikovsky. Story by V.P. Begitchev and Vasily Geltzer. First performed at the Bolshoi Theatre, Moscow, March, 1877. This version was unsuccessful and was revised by Lev Ivanov and Marius Petipa. Their successful version is described here. It was first performed at the Maryinsky Theatre, St. Petersburg, February, 1895.

Act One

Prince Siegfried's twenty-first birthday party is being held in the castle grounds. Guests are talking and having fun. Siegfried enters and talks to Benno, his friend, and Wolfgang, his old teacher.

Two girls and a boy dance a *pas de trois* for the guests, but Wolfgang is too busy drinking wine to notice. Siegfried's mother and her ladies enter. She is not pleased at the gaiety and reminds Siegfried that he is now a man and soon must choose a bride. Tomorrow night is the royal ball to celebrate Siegfried's birthday. She tells him that he is expected to choose a wife from one of the lovely ladies at his ball. Seeing that arguing will do no good, he agrees and leads his mother away.

Wolfgang is glad to see her go. He announces that, old as he is, he is still a better dancer than anyone else. Choosing a young girl as his partner, he throws himself into the dance. When he tries to whirl his partner around too many times, he loses his balance and they both fall down.

Siegfried returns and signals that the party should continue. More wine is served. He is determined not to think of tomorrow and his mother's orders. Benno, his friend, hears swans flying overhead and suggests that hunting will take Siegfried's mind off his problems.

Crossbows and flaming torches are brought for the hunting party. The village girls circle the stage and leave. Only old Wolfgang is unwilling to go hunting. He is too old, he says. The young men leave him behind with his bottle of wine.

Act Two

(This is the favorite act and is often performed as a shortened presentation of *Swan Lake*.)

Veronica Tennant as the Swan Queen and Raymond Smith as the Prince in The National Ballet of Canada production of *Swan Lake*.

The curtain rises on a beautiful lake in the forest. The hunting party enters and sees the swans nearby. When Siegfried arrives, the hunters tell him about the swans and rush off to the lake. Siegfried is about to follow when he notices something in the woods. He hides and watches it come his way.

It is the Queen of the Swans, who is half girl and half swan. She poses in *arabesque*, then bends her cheek down to her shoulder, just like a real swan. The Prince is touched by her loveliness and comes out of hiding.

The Swan Queen is frantic. She beats her arms, moving backward on point. When Siegfried asks why she is afraid, she points to his bow. He tells her that he would never harm her and that he is in love with her.

He wants to know who she is and why she is half girl and half swan. She is Odette, Queen of the Swans. The lake was made by her mother's tears when von Rotbart, the evil magician, turned Odette into the Swan Queen. Between midnight and dawn, she is a girl, but the rest of the time she must be a swan until someone promises to love her, marry her and never love another girl.

Siegfried tells her that he will save her. He asks where von Rotbart is. Just then, von Rotbart appears. His face is evil. With his long claws, he beckons Odette back to him. Siegfried aims his bow at von Rotbart, but Odette places herself in front of the bow, in *arabesque*, and asks for Siegfried's mercy. Von Rotbart disappears.

Siegfried holds the Swan Queen and tells her that she must come to his ball. He can then choose her for his wife, and the spell will be broken. Odette says no. She cannot come, for until she is married, von Rotbart has power over her. At the ball he would tell everyone her secret. She tells Siegfried that the magician will try to make him break his promise to her and, if he is successful, she will die.

The lovers leave and Odette's subjects, who are also girls from midnight until dawn, dance away from the lake. Benno, the Prince's friend, finds them. They rush past him as he calls the other huntsmen. The hunters aim their bows at the swans just as Odette and Siegfried return. She runs and stands in front of the swans to protect them, while Siegfried tells the men to put down their bows. When he explains the spell to the huntsmen, they bow in apology to the lovely young women.

Siegfried, Odette and the huntsmen leave. In one of the most charming parts of any ballet, the swans dance. Siegfried and Benno return to the scene and are joined by Odette. She touches Benno's shoulder and poses in *arabesque*, then rising on point, sinks slowly to the ground. Resting on one knee, her other leg stretched forward, she bends down low. Her arms come forward like swan's wings. Siegfried then joins her for an *adage*. The *adage* ends and we see dawn approaching.

Von Rotbart appears, beckoning the maidens back to the lake. Siegfried does not want Odette to go, but she must, promising to return. The huntsmen and Benno stand by the Prince and console him as Odette and the swans fly away.

ACT THREE

It is the following evening, and we are in the great hall of Siegfried's castle. The ball is about to take place.

Siegfried and his mother enter and sit on their high thrones. Ambassadors from foreign lands arrive and bow to the royal family. Six beautiful girls, all invited by Siegfried's mother, come before the throne. Although they are very pretty and wear beautiful gowns, Siegfried pays little attention to them. He is thinking of Odette.

His mother reminds him that he is supposed to dance with his beautiful guests. Half-heartedly, he goes from one to another and then quickly back to his throne. His mother is in the middle of scolding him for being rude when a knight and his daughter enter the hall. She is so lovely that Siegfried's mother allows her to come up to the thrones. Siegfried is excited. He thinks it is Odette.

Unknown to Siegfried, it is really Odile, von Rotbart's daughter.

The knight is none other than von Rotbart himself. Siegfried takes Odile into the garden while von Rotbart charms the Queen.

Now the guests from faraway lands – Spain, Hungary and Poland – perform their national dances for the entertainment of the other guests. When this series of dances ends, von Rotbart tells the Queen that his daughter is, by far, the best dancer at the ball.

Siegfried and Odile return and perform a *pas de deux*. Unlike the tender *adage* danced by Siegfried and Odette, this performance is full of pride, as Odile shows how well she can dance. Several times she goes to her father for instructions on even more movements that will charm Siegfried. She is cold and proud, but Siegfried still believes that she is Odette.

As the dramatic *pas de deux* continues, Odette appears in the window. She pleads with Siegfried, but Odile blocks his view. He does not see Odette. She disappears when Siegfried kneels before Odile, who stands above him in a conquering *arabesque*. The dance is over.

Siegfried is hopelessly captivated and asks the disguised von Rotbart for permission to marry his daughter. Von Rotbart quickly accepts, but asks Siegfried to vow that he will never love another girl. For a moment Siegfried hesitates. He has heard that request before and wonders why he should be asked again. Finally, as he says yes, there is a crash of thunder and the hall goes dark. In flashes of lightning, we see the guests running in fear while von Rotbart and his daughter stand laughing at their triumph. In the distance, Siegfried sees the heartbroken Odette and, realizing what has happened, falls to the floor.

ACT FOUR

At the lake, Odette and her swan maidens gather. The maidens try to console Odette, but it is no use. She is doomed.

Siegfried enters and Odette hides among the swans. She does not want him to see her. But, as he comes closer, the swans part and Odette stands before him. He explains von Rotbart's trickery and vows his love for her alone. It is no use. Odette must die. Only by dying will she be free of von Rotbart.

Von Rotbart appears. Angry at Odette's decision and Siegfried's interference, he tries to use his magic power to make her leave Siegfried. But Odette and Siegfried's love for each other is too strong for him and he disappears.

Telling Siegfried that the only way she can love him forever is to die, she throws herself in the lake. Realizing that what she has said is true for him as well, he follows her and drowns himself. This destroys von Rotbart. Love has won.

As the swan maidens dance farewell to their queen, Siegfried and Odette are seen on the lake. Now they are together forever.

BALLET NOTEBOOK
Ballet performances I have attended:

Date	Name of Ballet	Ballet Company	Theater

Ballet performances I have given:

ate	My Role	My School	Auditorium/Theater

PHOTOGRAPHY CREDITS

All photographs are by the author with the exception of the following: Miller Services, 100 (left), 101 (below); courtesy of The National Ballet of Canada, 100 (above), 101 (above left); Andrew Oxenham, The National Ballet of Canada, 16, 109, 113, 119, 121, 123; John Reeves, 10; David Street, 101 (above right); Martha Swope Photography, 104, 107, 115, 116.